50 Traditional Cooking of Japan's Snow Country

By: Kelly Johnson

Table of Contents

- Hegisoba (Seaweed-Bound Soba)
- Nozawana Tsukemono (Pickled Nozawana Greens)
- Yukimi Zake (Warm Sake with Snow Views)
- Kiritanpo Nabe (Toasted Rice Stick Hot Pot)
- Iburigakko (Smoked Pickled Daikon)
- Akita Komachi Rice Dishes
- Yonezawa Beef Sukiyaki
- Sasa Dango (Bamboo-Wrapped Sweet Dumplings)
- Nanban Miso (Spicy Miso Paste)
- Kanazawa Jibuni (Duck and Wheat-Gluten Stew)
- Oyaki (Stuffed Buckwheat Dumplings)
- Yuki Usagi Manju (Snow Rabbit Steamed Buns)
- Inaniwa Udon (Thin Hand-Stretched Udon)
- Sakata Sasa Sushi (Leaf-Wrapped Pressed Sushi)
- Doburoku (Unfiltered Sake)
- Noppe (Thick Root Vegetable Stew)
- Koya Dofu (Freeze-Dried Tofu)
- Echigo Mochi (Niigata Rice Cakes)
- Jinenjo Tororo (Grated Wild Yam Over Rice)
- Yamagata Dashi (Chilled Vegetable Condiment)
- Tazawako Smoked Trout
- Kanroni (Sweet Soy-Simmered Fish)
- Miso Grilled Hinai Jidori Chicken
- Hoshigaki (Dried Persimmons)
- Yukiguni Apple Pie
- Aizu Miso Dengaku (Grilled Miso Skewers)
- Sake Lees Hot Pot
- Sasazushi (Bamboo Leaf Sushi)
- Gintsuba (Sweet Bean Paste Cake)
- Kabocha Jiru (Pumpkin Miso Soup)
- Echigo Salmon Nabe (Snow Country Salmon Hot Pot)
- Suttate Jiru (Ground Sesame and Miso Soup)
- Burdock Tempura
- Snow Crab Donburi
- Oshizushi (Pressed Sushi)

- Tarako Mochi Soup (Salted Cod Roe Rice Cake Soup)
- Kinoko Gohan (Mushroom Rice)
- Zao Cheese Dishes
- Warabi Mochi (Bracken Starch Jelly)
- Hot Yam Soba
- Ichigo Daifuku (Strawberry-Filled Mochi)
- Dried Herring Nimono (Simmered Herring)
- Niigata Cod Roe Pasta
- Karinto (Sweet Fried Dough Sticks)
- Shonai Squid Sashimi
- Akita Sandfish Yaki
- Aizu Soba Gaki (Buckwheat Dumplings)
- Genmai Miso Soup (Brown Rice Miso Soup)
- Hokkaido Butter Corn Ramen
- Dobin Mushi (Matsutake Mushroom Broth in a Teapot)

Hegisoba (Seaweed-Bound Soba)

Ingredients

- 200g soba noodles
- 1 tbsp funori seaweed (rehydrated and blended)
- 4 cups dashi broth
- 2 tbsp soy sauce
- 1 tbsp mirin
- 1/2 tsp salt
- Green onions, sliced (for garnish)

Instructions

1. Boil soba noodles according to package instructions, then rinse in cold water.
2. In a pot, combine dashi, soy sauce, mirin, and salt. Heat to a simmer.
3. Serve soba chilled with dipping sauce or hot in broth, garnished with green onions.

Nozawana Tsukemono (Pickled Nozawana Greens)

Ingredients

- 200g nozawana greens, chopped
- 1 tbsp salt
- 1 tbsp rice vinegar
- 1 tsp sugar
- 1 dried chili (optional)

Instructions

1. Massage salt into nozawana and let sit for 30 minutes.
2. Rinse and squeeze out excess water.
3. Mix vinegar, sugar, and chili, then combine with greens.
4. Store in the fridge for at least 1 day before serving.

Yukimi Zake (Warm Sake with Snow Views)

Ingredients

- 1 cup sake
- 1 tbsp honey (optional)

Instructions

1. Gently warm sake in a pot until steaming (do not boil).
2. Stir in honey if desired.
3. Serve in a small cup and enjoy while watching the snowfall.

Kiritanpo Nabe (Toasted Rice Stick Hot Pot)

Ingredients

- 2 cups cooked rice
- 500g chicken thighs, sliced
- 4 cups dashi broth
- 1/2 cup burdock root, sliced
- 1/2 cup mushrooms
- 1/2 cup leeks, sliced
- 2 tbsp soy sauce
- 1 tbsp mirin
- 1/2 tsp salt

Instructions

1. Mash cooked rice and shape into cylindrical sticks around skewers.
2. Grill or pan-toast until slightly crispy.
3. In a pot, heat dashi, soy sauce, mirin, and salt.
4. Add chicken, burdock, mushrooms, and leeks, then simmer until cooked.
5. Add kiritanpo sticks at the end and serve hot.

Iburigakko (Smoked Pickled Daikon)

Ingredients

- 1 medium daikon radish
- 1 tbsp salt
- 2 tbsp rice vinegar
- 1 tbsp sugar
- 1 small piece smoked wood (for smoking)

Instructions

1. Rub daikon with salt and let sit for 1 day.
2. Rinse and soak in vinegar and sugar for 1 day.
3. Smoke over low heat for 1–2 hours.
4. Slice and serve as a side dish.

Akita Komachi Rice Dishes

Ingredients

- 2 cups Akita Komachi rice
- 4 cups water

Instructions

1. Rinse rice and soak for 30 minutes.
2. Cook using a rice cooker or stovetop until tender.
3. Serve with grilled fish, miso soup, or pickles.

Yonezawa Beef Sukiyaki

Ingredients

- 200g Yonezawa beef, thinly sliced
- 1/2 cup tofu, cubed
- 1/2 cup shiitake mushrooms
- 1/2 cup leeks, sliced
- 1/2 cup shirataki noodles
- 2 tbsp soy sauce
- 1 tbsp mirin
- 1 tbsp sugar
- 1/2 cup dashi broth
- 1 raw egg (for dipping)

Instructions

1. In a pan, heat dashi, soy sauce, mirin, and sugar.
2. Add beef, tofu, mushrooms, leeks, and noodles, cooking gently.
3. Serve hot, dipping pieces into raw egg before eating.

Sasa Dango (Bamboo-Wrapped Sweet Dumplings)

Ingredients

- 1 cup glutinous rice flour
- 1/2 cup water
- 1/4 cup red bean paste
- 4 bamboo leaves

Instructions

1. Mix rice flour and water into a smooth dough.
2. Wrap small portions of dough around red bean paste.
3. Wrap each dumpling in a bamboo leaf and secure with string.
4. Steam for 20 minutes until firm.

Nanban Miso (Spicy Miso Paste)

Ingredients

- 1/2 cup miso paste
- 1 tbsp chili flakes
- 1 tbsp mirin
- 1 tbsp soy sauce
- 1 tsp sugar

Instructions

1. Mix all ingredients in a bowl.
2. Store in an airtight container.
3. Use as a condiment for rice or grilled meats.

Kanazawa Jibuni (Duck and Wheat-Gluten Stew)

Ingredients

- 200g duck breast, sliced
- 1/2 cup wheat gluten (fu)
- 2 cups dashi broth
- 2 tbsp soy sauce
- 1 tbsp mirin
- 1 tbsp flour (for coating duck)

Instructions

1. Coat duck slices in flour.
2. In a pot, heat dashi, soy sauce, and mirin.
3. Add duck and wheat gluten, simmering until cooked.
4. Serve hot.

Oyaki (Stuffed Buckwheat Dumplings)

Ingredients

- 1 cup buckwheat flour
- 1/2 cup water
- 1/4 cup red bean paste or vegetable filling

Instructions

1. Mix flour and water into a dough.
2. Roll into small circles and fill with red bean paste or vegetables.
3. Pan-fry until golden, then steam for 10 minutes.
4. Serve warm.

Yuki Usagi Manju (Snow Rabbit Steamed Buns)

Ingredients

- 1 cup cake flour
- 1/4 cup sugar
- 1/2 tsp baking powder
- 1/4 cup water
- 1/2 cup red bean paste
- Red food coloring (for eyes)

Instructions

1. Mix flour, sugar, and baking powder. Slowly add water to form a dough.
2. Divide and flatten into small rounds.
3. Place red bean paste in the center, then seal and shape into ovals.
4. Use a toothpick to dab red food coloring as eyes.
5. Steam for 10 minutes until soft.

Inaniwa Udon (Thin Hand-Stretched Udon)

Ingredients

- 2 cups all-purpose flour
- 1/2 tsp salt
- 3/4 cup water

Instructions

1. Mix flour and salt, slowly adding water to form a dough.
2. Knead for 10 minutes, then rest for 2 hours.
3. Roll dough out, cut into thin strips, and stretch gently.
4. Boil for 2 minutes, then rinse in cold water.
5. Serve hot in broth or chilled with dipping sauce.

Sakata Sasa Sushi (Leaf-Wrapped Pressed Sushi)

Ingredients

- 2 cups cooked sushi rice
- 6 slices mackerel or salmon
- 6 bamboo leaves
- 2 tbsp rice vinegar

Instructions

1. Lightly press rice into small rectangular molds.
2. Top with fish and press gently.
3. Wrap each piece with a bamboo leaf.
4. Let sit for a few hours to absorb flavors before serving.

Doburoku (Unfiltered Sake)

Ingredients

- 2 cups cooked rice
- 4 cups water
- 1/2 cup koji rice
- 1/4 tsp yeast

Instructions

1. Mix cooked rice, water, koji, and yeast in a sterilized container.
2. Cover with a cloth and ferment at room temperature for 7–10 days, stirring daily.
3. Strain or enjoy unfiltered as doburoku.

Noppe (Thick Root Vegetable Stew)

Ingredients

- 1/2 cup taro, diced
- 1/2 cup carrots, diced
- 1/2 cup shiitake mushrooms, sliced
- 2 cups dashi broth
- 1 tbsp soy sauce
- 1 tbsp mirin
- 1/2 tbsp potato starch (for thickening)

Instructions

1. Simmer taro, carrots, and mushrooms in dashi for 15 minutes.
2. Stir in soy sauce and mirin.
3. Dissolve starch in water and stir into the stew to thicken.
4. Serve warm.

Koya Dofu (Freeze-Dried Tofu)

Ingredients

- 1 block firm tofu
- 2 cups dashi broth
- 1 tbsp soy sauce
- 1 tbsp mirin

Instructions

1. Freeze tofu overnight, then thaw and squeeze out excess water.
2. Simmer in dashi, soy sauce, and mirin for 10 minutes.
3. Serve warm or chilled.

Echigo Mochi (Niigata Rice Cakes)

Ingredients

- 1 cup glutinous rice flour
- 1/2 cup water
- 1/4 cup kinako (roasted soybean flour)
- 2 tbsp sugar

Instructions

1. Mix rice flour and water into a dough.
2. Steam for 10 minutes, then knead until smooth.
3. Shape into small cakes and coat with kinako mixed with sugar.

Jinenjo Tororo (Grated Wild Yam Over Rice)

Ingredients

- 1 small jinenjo (wild yam)
- 1 tbsp soy sauce
- 1 tsp dashi
- 1 bowl cooked rice

Instructions

1. Peel and grate jinenjo into a sticky paste.
2. Mix with soy sauce and dashi.
3. Pour over rice and serve immediately.

Yamagata Dashi (Chilled Vegetable Condiment)

Ingredients

- 1/2 cup cucumber, diced
- 1/2 cup eggplant, diced
- 1/4 cup shiso leaves, chopped
- 1 tbsp soy sauce
- 1 tbsp dashi

Instructions

1. Mix all ingredients in a bowl.
2. Chill for at least 1 hour.
3. Serve over rice or tofu.

Tazawako Smoked Trout

Ingredients

- 1 whole trout, cleaned
- 1 tbsp salt
- 1 small piece wood (for smoking)

Instructions

1. Rub trout with salt and let sit for 1 hour.
2. Smoke over low heat for 1–2 hours until cooked through.
3. Serve as a side dish or flaked over rice.

Kanroni (Sweet Soy-Simmered Fish)

Ingredients

- 2 small fish (sardines or ayu)
- 1/2 cup soy sauce
- 1/2 cup mirin
- 1/4 cup sugar
- 1 cup dashi broth
- 1 small piece ginger, sliced

Instructions

1. In a pot, combine soy sauce, mirin, sugar, dashi, and ginger.
2. Add fish and bring to a simmer.
3. Cook over low heat for 30–40 minutes until the liquid reduces.
4. Serve warm with rice.

Miso Grilled Hinai Jidori Chicken

Ingredients

- 2 Hinai Jidori chicken thighs (or free-range chicken)
- 2 tbsp miso paste
- 1 tbsp sake
- 1 tbsp mirin
- 1 tsp sugar
- 1 tsp sesame oil

Instructions

1. Mix miso, sake, mirin, sugar, and sesame oil into a marinade.
2. Coat chicken and marinate for at least 1 hour.
3. Grill over medium heat until golden and cooked through.
4. Serve with a side of rice.

Hoshigaki (Dried Persimmons)

Ingredients

- 4 firm persimmons
- String for hanging

Instructions

1. Peel persimmons, leaving the stem intact.
2. Tie string around the stems and hang in a well-ventilated area for 4–6 weeks.
3. Gently massage the persimmons daily after the first week to soften.
4. Once dried and coated with natural sugar, serve sliced.

Yukiguni Apple Pie

Ingredients

- 2 apples, peeled and sliced
- 1/4 cup sugar
- 1 tsp cinnamon
- 1 tbsp lemon juice
- 1 pre-made pie crust
- 1 egg yolk (for brushing)

Instructions

1. Preheat oven to 180°C (350°F).
2. Mix apples with sugar, cinnamon, and lemon juice.
3. Fill pie crust with apple mixture and cover with another layer of crust.
4. Brush with egg yolk and bake for 30–35 minutes until golden.

Aizu Miso Dengaku (Grilled Miso Skewers)

Ingredients

- 4 skewers of konnyaku, tofu, or eggplant
- 2 tbsp miso paste
- 1 tbsp mirin
- 1 tsp sugar
- 1/2 tsp sesame seeds

Instructions

1. Mix miso, mirin, and sugar into a thick paste.
2. Grill skewers until lightly charred.
3. Brush with miso glaze and sprinkle with sesame seeds.
4. Serve hot.

Sake Lees Hot Pot

Ingredients

- 200g thinly sliced pork or salmon
- 4 cups dashi broth
- 2 tbsp sake lees (sake kasu)
- 1 tbsp miso paste
- 1/2 cup napa cabbage, chopped
- 1/2 cup mushrooms
- 1/2 block tofu, cubed

Instructions

1. Dissolve sake lees and miso in dashi broth.
2. Add cabbage, mushrooms, and tofu, then simmer for 5 minutes.
3. Add pork or salmon and cook until done.
4. Serve warm.

Sasazushi (Bamboo Leaf Sushi)

Ingredients

- 2 cups cooked sushi rice
- 6 slices pickled fish (salmon or mackerel)
- 6 bamboo leaves
- 2 tbsp rice vinegar

Instructions

1. Lightly press rice into small rectangular molds.
2. Top with fish and press gently.
3. Wrap each piece with a bamboo leaf.
4. Let sit for a few hours before serving.

Gintsuba (Sweet Bean Paste Cake)

Ingredients

- 1 cup sweet red bean paste
- 1 cup all-purpose flour
- 1/2 cup water
- 1 tbsp sugar

Instructions

1. Mix flour, water, and sugar into a batter.
2. Spread a thin layer in a heated non-stick pan.
3. Add red bean paste and cover with another layer of batter.
4. Cook until golden on both sides.

Kabocha Jiru (Pumpkin Miso Soup)

Ingredients

- 1/2 cup kabocha pumpkin, diced
- 2 cups dashi broth
- 1 tbsp miso paste
- 1/2 cup tofu, cubed
- 1/4 cup green onions, sliced

Instructions

1. Bring dashi broth to a boil.
2. Add kabocha and simmer until soft.
3. Stir in miso and add tofu.
4. Serve with green onions.

Echigo Salmon Nabe (Snow Country Salmon Hot Pot)

Ingredients

- 200g salmon fillet, sliced
- 4 cups dashi broth
- 1/2 cup napa cabbage, chopped
- 1/2 cup mushrooms
- 1/2 block tofu, cubed
- 1 tbsp soy sauce
- 1 tbsp mirin

Instructions

1. Heat dashi broth and add soy sauce and mirin.
2. Add cabbage, mushrooms, and tofu, simmering for 5 minutes.
3. Add salmon and cook until done.
4. Serve hot.

Suttate Jiru (Ground Sesame and Miso Soup)

Ingredients

- 2 cups dashi broth
- 2 tbsp miso paste
- 2 tbsp ground sesame seeds
- 1/2 cup tofu, cubed
- 1/4 cup green onions, sliced

Instructions

1. Bring dashi broth to a simmer.
2. Stir in miso paste and ground sesame until dissolved.
3. Add tofu and cook for 3 minutes.
4. Serve garnished with green onions.

Burdock Tempura

Ingredients

- 1 burdock root, julienned
- 1/2 cup tempura flour
- 1/2 cup cold water
- 1 egg yolk
- Vegetable oil (for frying)

Instructions

1. Soak burdock in water for 10 minutes, then drain.
2. Mix tempura flour, water, and egg yolk.
3. Dip burdock in batter and deep-fry at 170°C (340°F) until golden.
4. Drain and serve with tempura sauce.

Snow Crab Donburi

Ingredients

- 1 cup cooked rice
- 100g snow crab meat
- 1 tbsp soy sauce
- 1 tbsp mirin
- 1/2 tsp wasabi (optional)
- 1/4 sheet nori, shredded

Instructions

1. Mix crab meat with soy sauce and mirin.
2. Serve over rice, garnished with wasabi and nori.

Oshizushi (Pressed Sushi)

Ingredients

- 2 cups cooked sushi rice
- 6 slices mackerel or salmon
- 2 tbsp rice vinegar
- 1 oshibako (wooden sushi mold)

Instructions

1. Lightly press rice into the mold.
2. Top with fish and press again.
3. Slice and serve.

Tarako Mochi Soup (Salted Cod Roe Rice Cake Soup)

Ingredients

- 2 cups dashi broth
- 2 tbsp tarako (salted cod roe)
- 2 mochi pieces
- 1 tbsp soy sauce
- 1/4 cup green onions, sliced

Instructions

1. Heat dashi broth and add soy sauce.
2. Add tarako and simmer for 2 minutes.
3. Grill mochi until soft, then add to the soup.
4. Serve hot with green onions.

Kinoko Gohan (Mushroom Rice)

Ingredients

- 2 cups short-grain rice
- 1/2 cup mixed mushrooms (shiitake, enoki, maitake)
- 2 tbsp soy sauce
- 1 tbsp mirin
- 2 cups dashi broth

Instructions

1. Rinse rice and drain.
2. Mix soy sauce, mirin, and dashi with rice.
3. Add mushrooms and cook as usual.
4. Let rest before serving.

Zao Cheese Dishes

Ingredients

- 100g Zao cheese (or mild white cheese)
- Crackers or bread for serving

Instructions

1. Slice cheese and serve with crackers or bread.
2. Optionally, melt over grilled vegetables or meat.

Warabi Mochi (Bracken Starch Jelly)

Ingredients

- 1/2 cup warabi starch
- 2 cups water
- 1/4 cup sugar
- 1/2 cup kinako (roasted soybean flour)

Instructions

1. Mix starch, water, and sugar in a pot.
2. Stir constantly over medium heat until thick.
3. Pour into a mold and cool.
4. Slice and coat with kinako before serving.

Hot Yam Soba

Ingredients

- 200g soba noodles
- 2 cups dashi broth
- 1 tbsp soy sauce
- 1/2 cup grated yam (tororo)
- 1/4 cup green onions, sliced

Instructions

1. Boil soba and drain.
2. Heat dashi with soy sauce.
3. Serve soba in broth, topped with grated yam and green onions.

Ichigo Daifuku (Strawberry-Filled Mochi)

Ingredients

- 1 cup glutinous rice flour
- 1/2 cup water
- 1/4 cup sugar
- 4 strawberries
- 1/2 cup sweet red bean paste

Instructions

1. Mix rice flour, sugar, and water. Microwave until thick.
2. Dust hands with cornstarch and flatten dough into rounds.
3. Wrap red bean paste and a strawberry inside.
4. Serve fresh.

Dried Herring Nimono (Simmered Herring)

Ingredients

- 2 dried herring fillets, soaked overnight
- 2 cups dashi broth
- 2 tbsp soy sauce
- 1 tbsp mirin
- 1 tbsp sake
- 1 tbsp sugar
- 1 small piece ginger, sliced

Instructions

1. Drain soaked herring and cut into portions.
2. In a pot, bring dashi, soy sauce, mirin, sake, sugar, and ginger to a simmer.
3. Add herring and cook over low heat for 30–40 minutes.
4. Serve warm with rice.

Niigata Cod Roe Pasta

Ingredients

- 200g spaghetti
- 2 tbsp tarako (cod roe)
- 2 tbsp butter
- 1 tbsp soy sauce
- 1 tbsp heavy cream (optional)
- Nori strips (for garnish)

Instructions

1. Cook spaghetti and drain.
2. In a bowl, mix cod roe, butter, soy sauce, and cream.
3. Toss pasta with the sauce until coated.
4. Garnish with nori before serving.

Karinto (Sweet Fried Dough Sticks)

Ingredients

- 1 cup all-purpose flour
- 2 tbsp sugar
- 1/4 tsp baking powder
- 2 tbsp water
- 1 tbsp sesame seeds (optional)
- Vegetable oil (for frying)
- 1/4 cup brown sugar (for coating)

Instructions

1. Mix flour, sugar, baking powder, and water into a dough.
2. Roll into thin sticks and deep-fry until golden.
3. Melt brown sugar in a pan with 1 tbsp water, then coat fried sticks.
4. Let cool before serving.

Shonai Squid Sashimi

Ingredients

- 1 fresh squid, cleaned
- 1 tbsp soy sauce
- 1 tsp wasabi
- 1 tbsp shiso leaves, chopped

Instructions

1. Slice squid into thin strips.
2. Serve with soy sauce, wasabi, and shiso leaves.

Akita Sandfish Yaki

Ingredients

- 2 Akita sandfish, cleaned
- 1 tbsp soy sauce
- 1 tbsp sake
- 1/2 tsp salt
- 1/2 lemon (for serving)

Instructions

1. Rub fish with salt and let sit for 10 minutes.
2. Grill over medium heat, brushing with soy sauce and sake.
3. Serve with a lemon wedge.

Aizu Soba Gaki (Buckwheat Dumplings)

Ingredients

- 1 cup buckwheat flour
- 1 cup water
- 1/4 tsp salt

Instructions

1. In a pot, bring water to a boil.
2. Gradually stir in buckwheat flour, mixing until thick.
3. Shape into small dumplings and serve warm.

Genmai Miso Soup (Brown Rice Miso Soup)

Ingredients

- 1/2 cup cooked brown rice
- 2 cups dashi broth
- 1 tbsp miso paste
- 1/2 cup tofu, cubed
- 1/4 cup green onions, sliced

Instructions

1. Heat dashi broth and stir in miso paste.
2. Add tofu and brown rice, simmering for 5 minutes.
3. Serve garnished with green onions.

Hokkaido Butter Corn Ramen

Ingredients

- 200g ramen noodles
- 3 cups chicken broth
- 1 tbsp miso paste
- 2 tbsp butter
- 1/2 cup corn kernels
- 1/4 cup green onions, sliced

Instructions

1. Cook ramen noodles and drain.
2. In a pot, heat chicken broth and miso paste.
3. Add butter and corn, stirring until melted.
4. Serve noodles in broth, topped with green onions.

Dobin Mushi (Matsutake Mushroom Broth in a Teapot)

Ingredients

- 2 cups dashi broth
- 1/2 cup matsutake mushrooms, sliced
- 1 shrimp, peeled
- 1/2 tsp soy sauce
- 1 small piece yuzu peel

Instructions

1. Bring dashi broth to a simmer and add mushrooms, shrimp, and soy sauce.
2. Cook for 5 minutes, then pour into a teapot.
3. Serve hot with yuzu peel garnish.

www.ingramcontent.com/pod-product-compliance
Lightning Source LLC
LaVergne TN
LVHW081506060526
838201LV00056BA/2959